YOUR KNOWLEDGE HAS VALUE

The implementation of artificial intelligence from an economic perspective and its social-ethic challenges

Marina Laukes

Bibliographic information published by the German National Library:

The German National Library lists this publication in the National Bibliography; detailed bibliographic data are available on the Internet at http://dnb.dnb.de.

ISBN: 9783346706201
This book is also available as an ebook.

Print and binding: Books on Demand GmbH, Norderstedt, Germany
Printed on acid-free paper from responsible sources.

The present work has been carefully prepared. Nevertheless, authors and publishers do not incur liability for the correctness of information, notes, links and advice as well as any printing errors.

GRIN web shop: https://www.grin.com/document/1265334

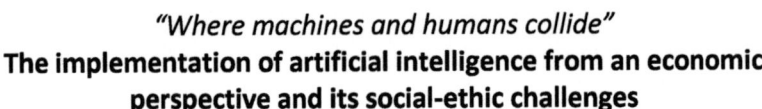

"Where machines and humans collide"
**The implementation of artificial intelligence from an economic
perspective and its social-ethic challenges**

Marina Laukes
THI Business School, Ingolstadt University of applied science Global Economics &
Business Management (B.A.)

Introduction

"Can machines think?" (Turing, 1950). With these pioneering words, and the questioning

in the so-called imitation game whether it enables machines to think autonomously, Alan M.

Turing developed one of the first fundamental ideas of machine learning and its significance for

the future as early as the 20th century. Machine learning (ML) or also known as Artificial

Intelligence (AI) is now no longer a dystopia that was only initially considered, it has evolved and is

a tangible reality and immeasurable in all aspects of life. Due to the fundamental paradigm shift,

massively marked by the emergence of digitalization and Industry 4.0, artificial intelligence, which

is being used almost across the board, will play a key role in the coming decades. The applicability

of artificial intelligence and increasingly complex algorithms continues to shape our everyday lives,

from smartphones and search engines to the financial and healthcare sectors. Beyond this, the use

of machine learning has a major impact on the economy and its future significant societal

implications. AI is a highly topical issue because, despite promising technological progress, the use

of AI is often controversial, especially with regard to whether the implementation of such

technology is morally and ethnically acceptable and whether certain legal and normative

boundaries are crossed. Therefore, the aim of this research paper is to analyze how far the

implementation of artificial intelligence will continue to have a decisive impact on economic

events and cause change. Irrespective of this, it is also important to analyze the social-ethnic

effects of the use of AI.

Defining AI

Defining the term "artificial intelligence" precisely is still unclear, as there is no uniform

explanation of the term due to the many different areas of application of AI, and it is also disputed

how to define the word intelligence itself. (Buxmann & Schmidt, 2019, p.6) An authoritative

definition that could endure for decades to come is that of Elaine Rich, whom she describes as

"Artificial Intelligence is the study of how to make computers do things at which, at the moment, people are better. " Conversely, this definition makes it clear that machine information processing

cannot exist without human cognitive thinking, which is why the boundaries between AI and

neuroscience are becoming increasingly blurred these days. (Ertel, 2017, p. 2, as cited in Rich,

1983) The term artificial intelligence can therefore no longer be categorized in any precise field of

research. Yet, artificial intelligence encompasses the field of computer science and aims to analyze

problem findings with stable data sets. Moreover, the term AI is often equated with machine

learning and deep learning, which in turn are a subfield of AI algorithms. (IBM Cloud Education,

2020). In particular, machine learning learns and makes decisions based on data that is already

available, and when so-called neural networks are added, this is called deep learning. Deep

Learning combines AI and Big Data (Menzel & Winkler, 2018) Symbolic AI follows a

phenomenological approach of human behavior, i.e., the knowledge and behavior of humans are

established in the intelligent systems, the learning process and the logic is very apparent. The

approach was considered promising for a while, but neural AI is on the rise. The neural AI or neural

networks manage in contrast to the symbolic large and unstructured data to evaluate, as well as

precise clustering to operate, thus intricate processes can be mastered. (Dickson, 2019) Not all

artificial intelligence is the same, there are key distinctions between weak and strong intelligence.

Basically, an AI is described as weak which, with the help of a targeted algorithm, takes on

individual tasks and separate problems. (James, 2019) Today, we are still in the realm of weak AI,

because systems like voice assistants, facial recognition systems or even autonomous vehicles fall

under the category of weak AI. (Labbe & Wigmore, n.d.) In contrast to weak AI, strong AI is still a

theory of the future, as it would mean that strong AI would have the full and congruent cognitive

abilities of a human. (IBM Cloud Education, 2020) The strong AI knows how to perfectly imitate the

human being with all his abilities. In addition, the strong AI should go so far as to analyze

knowledge transfer, future predictions based on previous knowledge, as well as adaptability in

changing situations in order to provide solutions. (James, 2019) How questionable and

fragmentary a super intelligence can be was already shown by an experiment from 2016:

Microsoft developed the AI chatbot Tay, which was placed on Twitter and had the task of learning from young people how they communicate. However, the premise here was that the bot had to be taken offline after only 24 hours because the bot was making Hitler comparisons, sexist remarks and Holocaust denials. (Hunt, 2016)

Applications of AI

The application of artificial intelligence is considerable and steadily increasing. AI is becoming commonplace. The most common keywords associated with AI are robotics or autonomous driving. However, sectors such as healthcare could benefit from the technology by improving diagnostics and optimizing medical interventions. AI could also contribute to sustainable optimization in the agricultural food industry, by analyzing data to minimize the use of fertilizer or water. Even in administrations and municipalities, AI could act as an early warning system of disasters. (Europäisches Parliament, 2020) The use of intelligent technology is also finding its way into industries and services. According to McKinsey (2020), AI is used significantly in product development and marketing, followed by personnel management and manufacturing. Figures also reflect usage, with 50% stating they have de-embedded AI in one of their business functions, and 22% of respondents reported that the use of AI accounted for 5% of their EBIT margin. (McKinsey, 2020)

Effect of AI on the Economy

The advancement of AI-based technologies is not diminishing, but accelerating, if not exponentially. In economic terms, AI is associated with the term general purpose technology, which can be understood as "there are a handful of "generic", or "general purpose" technologies (GPT' s) characterized by their pervasiveness (i.e., they can be used as inputs in a wide range of downstream sectors), and by their technological dynamism." (Bresnahan & Trajtenberg, 1992) As a result of the dramatic acceleration of AI, the implementation is also reflected in particular in the increase in financial resources. As a result of the dramatic acceleration of AI, the implementation is also reflected in particular in the increase in financial resources. Thus, the global venture capital of

AI start-ups rose from 3 billion US dollars in 2012 to 75 billion US dollars in 2020. About 80% of

these investments in 2020 are from China and the US, compared to only 4% from the EU. The

majority of investments were made in the automotive and transportation sectors, with China and

the United States accounting for almost 98%.(OCED, 2021) According to one estimate, the

implementation of AI could increase the value of global GDP to $15.7 trillion by 2030. (Firth-

Butterfield et al., 2022) In particular, China's immense investments in AI technologies are

remarkable. China's acceleration in AI technology is not just coming from nowhere, its regulations

on data protection are weak compared to the European market, and the use of AI-based facial

recognition programs has accelerated the Chinese market. (Li et al., 2021) In Germany, it is

assumed that only the adoption of AI technologies could increase the GDP by 11.3% by 2030,

which corresponds to 430 billion euros. (PWC, n.d.) Apart from the high investments made by

strong economic nations, the impact of AI on economic growth is debated repeatedly. The

assumption is that there are two main growth factors, one is direct GDP growth from companies

producing AI technology and the other is indirect GDP growth from sectors using AI to increase

productivity. (Chen et al., 2016) In the 1980s, the well-known economist Robert Solow put forward

the thesis of the productivity paradox. He argued that the age of information technology has no

discernible connection with a country's growth, but rather leads to stagnation. (Dudley, n.d.)

Solow's assumption may be confirmed, because the OCED also declares a decline in productivity in

the past years. The reasons for a slowdown in productivity growth are more far-reaching, because

on the one hand the effects of the financial crisis in 2008 are still having an impact, and on the

other hand the structural shift of the individual sectors influences growth, yet with the emergence

of the first commercially available computers at the end of the 1990s, the growth then associated

with them was declared insufficient. This in turn reflects Solow's assumption of the

complementarity of new technologies and productivity growth. (OCED economic outlook, 2019)

From a macroeconomic perspective, artificial intelligence could be another link in the so-called

production function. (Vöpel, 2018). The production function, which is composed of human capital, real capital, natural resources and technological knowledge, describes productivity. (Mankiw &

Taylor, 2016, p.679 – 681) Artificial intelligence increases the substitution function to human

capital, because the knowledge of the AI and its predicted abilities eliminate the knowledge and

qualification of the individuum. Due to the learning algorithms, the knowledge of the AI is

unbound, which illustrates the contrast to the bound human capital, which requires individual

learning and qualification. (Vöpel, 2018) If AI is included in the production function in combination

with Big Data, it would certainly be economically advantageous because returns could also be

skimmed off with it. (Schneider, 2021) Moreover, economists such as Brynjolfsson argue that,

despite all counterarguments, AI offers a way out of the productivity paradox in the long run,

precisely because AI acts as an additional intangible capital input. Hence, the assumption that the

handling of education and labor with respect to AI will no longer appear to be efficient in the

future and conventional measurements such as GDP will need to be adjusted. (Brynjolfsson, et al.,

2017) Furthermore, which is considered an economic and social controversy, is the question of

how the advancement of new technologies and the general aspect of automation endangers jobs.

From an economic point of view, it is very difficult to make a clear statement here, due to several

factors such as the rapid progress and changes in AI-based technologies, as the algorithms and

data volumes become increasingly powerful and large. (Buxmann & Schmidt, 2019, p. 30).

According to a study by the OCED (2021), only 14% of jobs are currently affected by automation,

which is also in contrast to the 12% increase in the labor market between 2012 and 2019.

Moreover, people with lower qualifications tend to be more affected by automation than those

with higher qualifications. (OCED, 2021) It is also estimated that about 85 million jobs will be

replaced by the year 2025 due to the shift in the labor market, but in turn 67 million new jobs will

be created through the interaction of humans and the algorithm. (World Economic Forum, 2020)

The insertion of AI into the production function shifts the relationship between labor and capital,

consequently weakening work with low skills, an example here would be the transport sector,

because the capital is there, but a significant reduction in labor. A capital less market entry of new competitors would be more efficient, because the data do not depend on capital, market entry

barriers are lowered. (Vöpel, 2018) The adaptation of AI is synonymous with efficiency and cost

savings in a wide range of industries. In fact, the use of AI is creating new economic orders, not

only in the entirely discussed showdown between machines and humans on the labor market, but

also in a wide range of industries. Economically, AI can be an asset and a driver of growth, labor

and capital, but any innovation is fraught with controversy, especially how to account for the

adaptation of AI ethnically and socially.

Social Challenges of AI

Due to the dynamic nature of AI technology, the controversy surrounding AI must be examined

from a social perspective. Although AI will only lead to a deferral of work and not to outright mass

unemployment, the social controversy surrounding technology and work centers on the fact that it

fosters the growth of social inequality. Thus, according to a scientific study, AI in the U.S. is

responsible for a reduction in wages of about 50% to 70%. The increasing inequality in wealth and

income is therefore brought with the automation, because while the salary of people with a higher

degree increased, in contrast, the salary of less qualified people decreased. (Kelly, 2021) In the

context of the inequality debate, human enhancement technologies play an essential role. The

assumption here is that intelligence is measurable. People with a higher income are measured

with a higher intelligence, a higher productivity, again the resulting dilemma is that the rest with a

lower income represents the opposite. Ultimately, incentives are created for the solvent part of

society, improvements can be easily bought, moreover, they are in competition with other

wealthy people. The fact is, there is a dependency between income and well-being. The majority

of society with low incomes who do not have access to the latest technologies are left behind. As a

result of the increasing dynamic of innovation growth, a void is emerging between the best

technologies and what is publicly obtainable for the poorer part of the population. (Korinek &

Stiglitz, 2017) Moreover, AI or rather the sub-discipline Machine Learning can contribute to

decision-making, but there is a risk that decisions will be cognitively biased. (Silberg & Manyika,

2019) As a result, the bias of the algorithm leads to major misunderstandings and even

discrimination. Thus, during the ML learning phase, certain and already existing social biases are

reinforced and even replicated. (Garcia-Gathright, et. al., 2018) In the past, large companies such

as Amazon.com used AI algorithms in the recruitment process to make the review of individual

CVs more efficient, but the algorithm caused a bias where women were treated less favorably in

the selection process. (Dilmegani, 2022) In addition, as with any new technology, there is of course

the question of the extent to which transparency and data protection are affected. To ensure safe

handling, some countries, including the European Union (2021), have already taken legislative

measures with reference to the emerging risks of AI. The framework is intended to be compatible

with EU fundamental rights and impacts both individuals and organizations. However, the current

non-transparency, otherwise known as the black box of AI, could further fuel the criticism,

because the so-called black box paradox is understood as the impenetrable system of any AI, in

short, inputs and executions are not visible. Due to this impenetrability of AI, biases also arise.

(Caussauwers, 2020) The extent to which AI affects privacy is also still controversial. China uses AI

to analyze the data collected from its citizens and ultimately to build a rating system for their

behavior. Here, transparency around AI receives a completely new dimension (Buxmann, 2018) AI

literally embodies the keywords transparency and above all privacy, so one often speaks of the so-

called AI dilemma. The dilemma is that AI feeds large amounts of data and the larger the amount

of data, the greater the risk of misuse. The original purposes are disregarded, data could be sold to

third parties or stolen. (Sträter & Lundbaek, 2021) Thus it is already in such a way that for the

personnel selection algorithms are used which act after the Black box principle, like which

selection criteria were met, remain thus obscure. (Buxmann, 2018) Weak AIs such as smart home

devices like Alexa or Google come under criticism frequently. It has long been known that voice

assistants record what their users say, some of it confidential, which is then stored in a cloud.

Therefore, it happens that in more than one out of ten protocols, Alexa accidentally went on.

(Lynskey, 2019) A trusting consensus must be established between machine and human, otherwise a social democracy is probably exposed to possible dangers. Besides the factor of using AI as a

surveillance tool, so-called deep fakes could contribute to a manipulation of society, because deep

fakes are still an impenetrability from a social point of view, but the danger of manipulation of

information media is increasing. (Bauberger, 2020, p.119) Deep fakes are based on neural

networks that are capable of faking text, audio, and movies. Deep Fakes allow changing or

recreate faces and facial expressions of an individuum without any great effort and with high

quality, so that, for instance, deceptive statements of a person are shown in a video, which,

however, never existed in reality. (BSI, n. d.) Deep fakes fuel disinformation, which in turn is an

obstacle to democracy. Deep fakes are becoming a hybrid warfare tool, and the current situation

demonstrates this all the more. In the conflict between Ukraine and Russia, a video of the

Ukrainian president explaining the capitulation to Russia in an alleged speech appeared. It was not

immediately obvious that this was a deep fake, but the signs such as the proportion of the head, as

well as a deeper voice spoke for it. (Wakefield, 2022) The threats of deep fakes are wide-ranging,

from manipulation of biometric identification procedures, to phishing attacks and targeted

spreading of disinformation. (BSI, n.d.) Furthermore, an experiment at Stanford University shows

how fine the line can be between using algorithms and weighing social morality. The experiment

shows that it is possible to recognize homosexuality on the basis of the face using neural networks

/deep learning. (Wang & Kosinski, 2017) Democracy and its basic principles are in contrast to

Artificial Intelligence and its doom of privacy and transparency, especially the data-intensive

opaque machine learning is in the public discourse of taking democracy out of control and making

society controllable to ultimately weaken it in the long run. (Hoffmann & Thiel, 2021)

Ethic and Law Issues

Moreover, the public discourse raises the moral-ethnic question of the extent to which it is

acceptable for algorithms to take over responsibility and completely replace the decision-making

of the human medium. The term technological singularity describes the notion of many that fully

intelligent machines are gaining such power that they exceed the capabilities of humans. However, at the current juncture, this is far from being achieved as we are still in the stage of a weak AI,

which is not comparable to the cognition of humans. (Talagala, 2021) At present, the fundamental

question of how far an algorithm may be equal to a human being can be illustrated by the

controversial topic of autonomous driving. AI makes analytical decisions where, in contrast,

humans rely on their intuition and rational trade only partially prevails. The implementation of AI

in autonomous driving is declared as an ethnic dilemma, because in the causality of accident and

death, debate arises to what extent an AI has the power to value one life higher than another.

(Reismann, 2021) With the conception of the so-called moral machine of MIT, which pursues the

goal of the Debate ethnics programming with the autonomous driving more hearing to make,

developed a computer model with which the participants a decision had to make, whether a child,

homeless person, older or animals, as well as social status and qualification included, which may

survive in the case of an accident. (Parsch, 2018) Autonomous driving is related to the statement

of how vehicles decide regarding a situation, but basically the decision is not made by the machine

as a subject. The decision is only as good as that of the programmed algorithm, so ethnic

decisions, especially this of autonomous driving, must be decided by humans with personal

accountability. (Bauberger, 2020, p.97) As a result, some countries are aware of the need for

ethnic enlightenment with regard to autonomous driving, including Germany, where an Ethics

Commission for Autonomous Driving has been established. Therefore, the ethics commission

introduces the following principles, such as that the human being and his/her self-responsible

decisions have top priority and those intelligent systems must not make any distinction in the

socio-demographic data in the event of an accident situation. (Bundesminsterium für Verkehr und

digitale Infrastruktur, 2017) Controversial is also the question whether it is ethnically justifiable,

especially with reference to human rights to use weapon with AI. Controversial is also the question

whether it is ethnically and above all morally justifiable, especially with regard to human rights, to

use weapons with AI. The arms race around AI weapons is highly contentious, because the main

argument is that AI-based weapons cannot distinguish who is a civilian, an attacker, or a fighter.

According to Human Rights Watch, about 30 countries have spoken out against AI weapons so far,

but only a few of them are in Europe. (Polistina, 2020) At the center of intelligent weapons is the

fundamental question of responsibility and the concept of morality and dignity. When a human life

is taken by a human being, this occurs in the consciousness of the human being and the

subsequent consequences, but if the killing is carried out by a machine with a programmed

algorithm, the question arises as to who takes responsibility for this. (Vagt, 2019) As a result, the

basic question of responsibility is diffused, because it is easier for humans, as the actual actors, to

avoid responsibility and leave it to the AI. (Bauberger, 2020, p.106) Beside the ethnic basic

thoughts there are also the legal ones, here it is to be questioned whether an AI can be declared as

a legal person. Some argue that intelligent systems should be recognized as e-persons, which again

would mean that robots would be liable or even legitimately punishable. (Wendehorst, 2020)

Recognizing an AI as an e-person would also mean that it would be entitled to legal obligations or

even transfer of property, which until now has been reserved for legal entities only, furthermore

the AI would have to be administratively recorded in a register as an e-person. (Pappenhage, 2022)

However, to recognize autonomous systema as a legal or e-person is to declare as a refusal. If

producers were free from any liability for their innovations, there would be no incentive for new

innovations and people's trust in technology would decrease, but too strict regulations would

reduce the incentive for innovation. (Europäisches Parlament, 2020) Furthermore, a rejection is

also necessary because algorithms constantly overwrite and optimize themselves through their

learning processes, which in turn contradicts the human being and this would only further

promote the moral-ethnic confusion. (Wendehorst, 2020) Ethics with reference to AI also means

including human values and norms. Dignity is the foundation of basic human needs such as

transparency, security, rights. However, the implementation of AI provides a shift here as well. As

explained, tools such as Deep Fakes can significantly modify the understanding of reason, of right

and wrong. The boundaries thus become blurred and the belief in values and norms is increasingly

doubted. The need for participation and recognition with the inclusion of algorithm in everyday life and especially the resulting bias can lead to a social discrepancy. (Al-Rodhan, 2021) Between

machine and human it is necessary for each country and government to develop a framework to

create clear boundaries to bring human rights in line with new technologies. The regulation Art. 2

ECHR the right of dignity and integrity of the human being, anchored in the European human

rights convention, must be put in such a way into the foreground that executed tasks by an

intelligent system do not impair the human being in his dignity and. In addition, it is important to

ensure transparent information transfer at all times in the event of interaction between man and

machine. (Leslie, et al., 2021) The fact is that machines and humans are becoming more and more

involved with each other, so in the long-term laws must be made with special attention to the

ethics that encompass the values and norms of the human individuum, because even scientists like

Stephen Hawking (2018, p. 212) point out that an adaptation of AI and its competence could be

socially the best or the worst.

Conclusion

On the whole, the introduction of artificial intelligence and its subdiscipline`s machine

learning and deep learning is leading to a fundamental and foreseeable change in society at all

levels, especially in the economic and ethnic consensus. Technologies around AI are leading to a

global arms race between the major powers, not for nothing massive investment offensives are

launched, which in turn also fuels the future geopolitical importance of AI and its subdisciplines.

However, new innovations are known to lead to division, as it remains questionable to what

extent Roberts Solow's assumption is consistent with the productivity paradox and new

technologies. However, the correlation between AI and productivity exists, because in the long

run, AI may substitute for labor and lead to a shift in sectors, although the exact impact on the

elimination of workers can be conjectured. Algorithm and data create a veritable data economy.

The questions of labor market, education, and competition form a new power vacuum. Thus, it is

possible that in the course of AI, correlations between competitiveness and prosperity will

emerge. Artificial intelligence is clearly revolutionizing the current economic order. However, the inequalities caused by labor-substituting technologies are increasing altogether, which in turn leads to a fragmentation of society. If preventive measures are not taken, the gap between the highly qualified income strata and the lower ones will continue to widen. But not only the emergence of inequalities reflects a possible resistance of society to AI, but also the question of transparency and trust. The distortion generated by algorithmic issues is really fueling people's mistrust instead of building a trustworthy consensus. AI must not become tools of instrumentalization. However, as with tools such as deep fakes or the black box principle, there is a risk that it will happen if laws are not established. Transparency, especially in the context of new technologies, creates a basis for the future continuity of new innovations. In order not to further fuel the expansion of inherent risks of AI, it is not enough that only rules or recommendations are issued, laws are needed, anchored in the legislature of each country. With regard to automated driving, as well as the possible use of intact weapon systems, laws are also needed to preserve the omnipresent fundamental principle of human dignity and freedom. Because the highest commandment is still to put the human before the machine. It is necessary with advancing development of the AI that the control is preserved and that a conscious acting of humans with consideration is established. Basically, the public discourse around AI must be fueled even more, it requires education regarding opportunities as well as the risks. Nevertheless, artificial intelligence and its subdisciplines can be such a wonderful tool, whether economically or even in everyday life, it is part of what will bring about positive change in many areas, if not even usher in a new era. Beyond that, interfaces between society as a whole, political and economic actors must be formed in order to bring the increasingly intelligent algorithms in line with human values and norms. To take up again the sentence "Can machines think?" by Turing (1950) - machines or AI are already a part of our society but it is still only a tool which benefits the optimization urge of humans, albeit one that will lead to a continuous transformation across generations. Merely in the up to which ridge this will happen, that decides the individual human, because the human has precedence before any machine intelligence.

References

Al-Rodhan, N. (2021, March 27). *Artificial Intelligence: Implications for human dignity and*

governance. https://oxfordpoliticalreview.com/2021/03/27/artificial-intelligence/

Bauberger, S. (2020). *Welche KI? Künstliche Intelligenz demokratisch gestalten.* Carl Hanser

Verlag.

Bresnahan, T. F. & Trajtenberg, M. (1992, August). *General Purpose Technologies: "Engines*

of growth?". https://www.nber.org/papers/w4148

Buxmann, P. & Schmidt, H. (2019). *Künstliche Intelligenz.* Springer Gabler.

Buxmann, P. (2018, December 08). *Der gläserne Mensch wird durch KI noch*

transparenter. https://ec.europa.eu/research-and-innovation/en/horizon-

magazine/opening-black-box-artificial-intelligence

Bundesministerium für Verkehr und digitale Infrastruktur. (2017, June). *Ethik Kommission*

automatisiertes und vernetztes Fahren.

https://www.bmvi.de/SharedDocs/DE/Publikationen/DG/bericht-der-ethik-

kommission.pdf?__blob=publicationFile

Bundesamt für Sicherheit in der Informationstechnik. (n.d.). *Deepfakes – Gefahren und*

Gegenmaßnahmen. https://www.bsi.bund.de/DE/Themen/Unternehmen-und-

Organisationen/Informationen-und-Empfehlungen/Kuenstliche-

Intelligenz/Deepfakes/deepfakes_node.html

Brynjolfsson, E., Rock, D., Syverson, C. (2017, November). *Artificial Intelligence and the*

modern productivity paradox: c clash of expectations and statistics.

https://www.nber.org/system/files/working_papers/w24001/w24001.pdf

Caussauwers, T. (2020, December 01). *Opening the 'black box' of artificial intelligence.*

https://ec.europa.eu/research-and-innovation/en/horizon-magazine/opening-black-box-artificial-

intelligence

Chen, N., Christensen, L., Gallagher, K., Mate, R., Rafert, G., (2016, February). *Global*

Economic Impacts Associated with Artificial Intelligence.

https://www.analysisgroup.com/globalassets/content/insights/publishing/ag_full_report_econom

ic_impact_of_ai.pdf

Dickson, B. (2019, November 18). *What is symbolic intelligence?*

https://bdtechtalks.com/2019/11/18/what-is-symbolic-artificial-intelligence/

Dilmegani, C., (September 12, 2020). *Bias in AI: What it is, Types, Examples & 6 Ways to Fix*

it in 2022. Retrieved 2022, April 3. https://research.aimultiple.com/ai-bias/

Dudley, S. (n.d.). *The Internet Just Isn't That Big a Deal Yet: A Hard Look at Solow's*

Paradox. https://www.wired.com/insights/2014/11/solows-paradox/

Ertel, W. (2017). *Introduction to Artificial Intelligence.* (2nd ed.). Springer.

Europäisches Parlament. (2020). Rahmen für die ethischen Aspekte von künstlicher Intelligenz,

Robotik und damit zusammenhängenden Technologien.

https://www.europarl.europa.eu/doceo/document/TA-9-2020-0275_DE.pdf

Europäische Parlament. (2020, September 14). *Was ist künstliche Intelligenz und wie wir*

sie genutzt?

https://www.europarl.europa.eu/news/de/headlines/society/20200827STO85804/was-ist-

kunstliche-intelligenz-und-wie-wird-sie-genutzt

Europäische Kommission. (2021, April 4). *Verordnung des Europäischen Parlaments und*

des Rates. https://eur-lex.europa.eu/legal-content/DE/TXT/?uri=CELEX%3A52021PC0206

Firth-Butterfield K., Tolpic, L., Anthony, A., Reid, E. (2022, March 19). *AI will add $15.7*

trillion to global GDP by 2030. Here are three ways to become 'literate'.

https://theprint.in/science/ai-will-add-15-7-trillion-to-global-gdp-by-2030-here-are-three-ways-to-

become-literate/879753/

Garcia-Gathright, J., Springer, A., Cramer, H. (September, 2018). *Assessing and Addressing*

Algorithmic Bias – But Before We Get There. https://arxiv.org/pdf/1809.03332.pdf

Hawking, S. (2018). *Kurze Antworten auf große Fragen*. Klett-Cotta.

Hoffmann, J., Thiel, T.(2021, March). *Schleichende Übernahme Künstliche Intelligenz und der Wandel der Demokratie*. https://bibliothek.wzb.eu/artikel/2021/f-23699.pdf

Hunt, E. (2016, March 24). *Tay, Microsoft's AI chatbot, gets a crash course in racism from Twitter*. https://www.theguardian.com/technology/2016/mar/24/tay-microsofts-ai-chatbot-gets-a-crash-course-in-racism-from-twitter

IBM Cloud Education. (2020, August 31). *Strong AI*. https://www.ibm.com/cloud/learn/strong-ai

IBM Cloud Education. (2019, 3 June). *Artificial Intelligence (AI)*. https://www.ibm.com/cloud/learn/what-is-artificial-intelligence

Kelly, J. (2021, June 18). Artificial Intelligence Has Caused A 50% To 70% Decrease In Wages—Creating Income Inequality And Threatening Millions Of Jobs. https://www.forbes.com/sites/jackkelly/2021/06/18/artificial-intelligence-has-caused--50-to-70-decrease-in-wages-creating-income-inequality-and-threatening-millions-of-jobs/?sh=3a6c6a9a1009

Korinek, A., Stiglitz, J. E. (2017, December). *Artificial Intelligence and its implication for income distribution and unemployment*. https://www.nber.org/system/files/working_papers/w24174/w24174.pdf

James, R. (2019, October 30). *Understanding Strong vs. Weak AI in a New Light*. https://becominghuman.ai/understanding-strong-vs-weak-ai-in-a-new-light-890e4b09da02

Labbe, M. & Wigmore, I. (n.d.) *narrow AI (weak AI)*. https://www.techtarget.com/searchenterpriseai/definition/narrow-AI-weak-AI

Leslie, D., Burr, C., Aitken, M., Cowls, J., Katell, M., Briggs, M. (2021). *AI, human rights, democracy and the rule of law: A primer prepared for the Council of Europe*. *https://www.turing.ac.uk/sites/default/files/2021-03/cahai_feasibility_study_primer_final.pdf*

Li, D., Tong, T. W., Xiao, Y. (February 18, 2021*). Is China Emerging as the Global Leader in

AI?* https://hbr.org/2021/02/is-china-emerging-as-the-global-leader-in-ai

Lynske, D. (2019, October 09). *'Alexa, are you invading my privacy?' – the dark side of our

voice assistants.* https://www.theguardian.com/technology/2019/oct/09/alexa-are-you-invading-

my-privacy-the-dark-side-of-our-voice-assistants

Mankiw, G. N., Taylor, M. P. (2016). *Grundzüge der Volkswirtschaftslehre.* (6nd ed.) Schäfer-

Poeschel Verlag Stuttgart.

McKinsey. (2020, November 19). *The state of AI in 2020.*

https://www.mckinsey.com/business-functions/mckinsey-analytics/our-insights/global-survey-

the-state-of-ai-in-2020

Menzel, C. & Winkler, C. (2018). *Zur Diskussion der Effekte Künstlicher

Intelligenz in der wirtschaftswissenschaftlichen Literatur.*

https://www.bmwi.de/Redaktion/DE/Downloads/Diskussionspapiere/20190205-

diskussionspapier-effekte-kuenstlicher-intelligenz-in-der-wirtschaftswissenschaftlichen-

literatur.pdf?__blob=publicationFile&v=6

OCED. (2021, April 4). *A sharp increase in AI-related venture capitalist investments could

transform global economies and shape the future of artificial intelligence.* https://oecd.ai/en/vc

OCED. (2019, January). *What happened to jobs at high risk of automation?*

*https://www.oecd.org/future-of-work/reports-and-data/what-happened-to-jobs-at-high-risk-of-

automation-2021.pdf*

OCED. (2019, May). *OCED Economic Outlook Volume 2019.* https://www.oecd-

ilibrary.org/sites/b2e897b0-en/1/2/2/index.html?itemId=/content/publication/b2e897b0-

en&_csp_=d2743ede274dd564946a04fc1f43d5dc&itemIGO=oecd&itemContentType=book

Pappenhagen, N. (2022, March 16). *Die Einführung der E-Person – absurdes

Gedankenexperiment oder realistisches Szenario?* https://www.rechtverblueffend.com/post/die-

einf%C3%BChrung-der-e-person-k%C3%BCnstliche-intelligenz

Parsch, S. (2018, October 24). *Kind oder Oma – wenn soll das autonome Auto bei Unfall*

verschonen? https://www.welt.de/gesundheit/psychologie/article182665856/Moral-Machine-

Mehrheit-wuerde-autonome-Autos-eher-gegen-Aeltere-lenken-lassen.html

Polistina, F. (2020, August 10). *Warnung vor den autonomen Killern.*

https://www.sueddeutsche.de/politik/kuenstliche-intelligenz-killerroboter-diplomatie-1.4994751

PWC, (n.d.). *Küsntliche Intelligenz sorgt für Wachsstumsschub.*

https://www.pwc.de/de/digitale-transformation/business-analytics/kuenstliche-intelligenz-sorgt-

fuer-wachstumsschub.html

Reismann, S. (2021, March 09). *Ethik für autonome Fahrzeuge – Wer soll sterben?*

https://www.netzpiloten.de/ethik-fuer-autonome-fahrzeuge/

Schneider, J. (2021, August 02). *Wieso künstliche Intelligenz das neue Kapital ist.*

https://www.ey.com/de_de/ai/kuenstliche-intelligenz-ist-das-neue-kapital

Sträter, R. & Lundbaek, L. (March, 2021). *The Ai privacy Dilemma.*

https://www.dotmagazine.online/issues/safeguarding-users-and-data/Europes-digital-data-

decade/the-ai-privacy-dilemma

Silberg, J., Manyika, J. (2019, June 6). *Tackling bias in artificial intelligence (and in humans).*

https://www.mckinsey.com/featured-insights/artificial-intelligence/tackling-bias-in-artificial-

intelligence-and-in-humans

Talagala, N. (2021, June 2021). *Don't Worry About The AI Singularity: The Tipping Point Is*

Already Here. https://www.forbes.com/sites/nishatalagala/2021/06/21/dont-worry-about-the-ai-

singularity-the-tipping-point-is-already-here/?sh=e2829171cd44

Turing, A. M. (2021). *Computing Machinery and Intelligence Können Maschinen Denken?*

Philipp Reclam jun. Verlag GbmbH.

Vagt, S. (2019, December 06). *Autonome Waffensysteme: Die Zukunft des Krieges.*

https://www.freiheit.org/de/autonome-waffensysteme-die-zukunft-des-krieges

Vöpel, H. (2018). *Wie künstliche Intelligenz die Ordnung der Wirtschaft revolutioniert.*

https://www.wirtschaftsdienst.eu/inhalt/jahr/2018/heft/11/beitrag/wie-kuenstliche-intelligenz-

die-ordnung-der-wirtschaft-revolutioniert.html

Wakefield, J. (2022, March 18). *Deepfake presidents use in Russia-Ukraine war.*

https://www.bbc.com/news/technology-60780142

Wang, Y., Kosinski, M. (2017). *Deep neural networks can detect sexual orientation from.*

https://www.gsb.stanford.edu/sites/default/files/publication-pdf/wang_kosinski.pdf

Wendehorst, C. (2020, January 13). *Ist ein Roboter haftbar? https://www.forschung-und-*

lehre.de/recht/ist-ein-roboter-haftbar-2415

World Economic Forum. (October, 2020). *The future of jobs report 2020.*

https://www3.weforum.org/docs/WEF_Future_of_Jobs_2020.pdf